NORTH AMERICAN NATURAL RESOURCES

IRON

North American Natural Resources

Coal

Copper

Freshwater Resources

Gold and Silver

Iron

Marine Resources

Natural Gas

Oil

Renewable Energy

Salt

Timber and Forest Products

Uranium

NORTH AMERICAN NATURAL RESOURCES

IRON

John Perritano

MASON CREST

Mason Crest
450 Parkway Drive, Suite D
Broomall, PA 19008
www.masoncrest.com

MTM Publishing, Inc.
435 West 23rd Street, #8C
New York, NY 10011
www.mtmpublishing.com

President: Valerie Tomaselli
Vice President, Book Development: Hilary Poole
Designer: Annemarie Redmond
Illustrator: Richard Garratt
Copyeditor: Peter Jaskowiak
Editorial Assistant: Andrea St. Aubin

Series ISBN: 978-1-4222-3378-8
ISBN: 978-1-4222-3383-2
Ebook ISBN: 978-1-4222-8557-2

Library of Congress Cataloging-in-Publication Data
Perritano, John.
  Iron / by John Perritano.
     pages cm. — (North American natural resources)
  Includes bibliographical references and index.
  ISBN 978-1-4222-3383-2 (hardback) — ISBN 978-1-4222-3378-8 (series) — ISBN
978-1-4222-8557-2 (ebook)
  1. Iron—Juvenile literature. 2. Steel—Juvenile literature. 3. Iron—Economic aspects—
Juvenile literature. 4. Iron—Environmental aspects—Juvenile literature. I. Title.
  QD181.F4P47 2015
  669'.141—dc23
                         2015005848

Printed and bound in the United States of America.

First printing
9 8 7 6 5 4 3 2 1

TABLE OF CONTENTS

Key Icons to Look for:

Words to Understand: These words with their easy-to-understand definitions will increase the reader's understanding of the text, while building vocabulary skills.

Sidebars: This boxed material within the main text allows readers to build knowledge, gain insights, explore possibilities, and broaden their perspectives by weaving together additional information to provide realistic and holistic perspectives.

Research Projects: Readers are pointed toward areas of further inquiry connected to each chapter. Suggestions are provided for projects that encourage deeper research and analysis.

Text-Dependent Questions: These questions send the reader back to the text for more careful attention to the evidence presented there.

Series Glossary of Key Terms: This back-of-the-book glossary contains terminology used throughout the series. Words found here increase the reader's ability to read and comprehend higher-level books and articles in this field.

Note to Educator: As publishers, we feel it's our role to give young adults the tools they need to thrive in a global society. To encourage a more worldly perspective, this book contains both imperial and metric measurements as well as references to a wider global context. We hope to expose the readers to the most common conversions they will come across outside of North America.

Major Iron Deposits in Use in North America, 2015

Major Iron Deposit
Site Mentioned in Text

Davis Strait

Hudson Bay

Labrador Trough

C A N A D A

Hull Rust Mahoning Mine   Mesabi Range

Hamilton, Ontario

Moriah, New York
Saugus Iron Works
Roxbury, Connecticut

U N I T E D   S T A T E S
O F   A M E R I C A

Canton, Ohio
Youngstown, Ohio   Pittsburgh, Pennsylvania

Gateway Arch

*ATLANTIC
OCEAN*

*PACIFIC
OCEAN*

M E X I C O

Gulf of Mexico

Caribbean Sea

0 km   500   1,000
0 miles   500

0 km   500   1,000   1,500
0 miles   500   1,000

INTRODUCTION

ron is a hard-working element. We put it in our bridges and in our skyscrapers. We build homes with iron fences to separate us from our neighbors. We take iron pills to make sure our body's organs work as they should. Your family may have an iron frying pan or even an iron kettle in the kitchen.

Iron plays a key role in architecture, such as the exteriors of these buildings in Soho, New York City. (Rifberlin/Dreamstime)

Easy to find and almost effortless to shape, humans have used iron to build great cities, create civilizations, and make their armies stronger. The earliest humans plucked pure iron from the meteorites they found, chiseling and sculpting it into tools, eating utensils, and weapons.

On its own, iron is hard and brittle. But when it is mixed with carbon, the result is steel, which we use to build everything from tools to buildings to satellites. Iron does present a few challenges, however. It is highly reactive. This means that when it is exposed to air or water, it begins to corrode, or rust. The mining of iron and the production of steel are often harmful to the environment. But at the same time, iron and steel are the backbone of many economies.

Chapter One

HISTORY

On a summer day in 1830, a significant and unique race was held. Peter Cooper's steam locomotive *Tom Thumb* raced a horse named Lighting. The two lined up side by side—*Tom Thumb* on its tracks, ready to pull a cartload of passengers, and Lighting with its hoofs on the ground, ready to pull its own cart. The starter fired a gun. The race was on.

Words to Understand

alloy: a mixture of two or more metals.

forge: to make or shape metal by heating it in a furnace, or by hammering it; also, a place where this process occurs.

indentured servants: workers who agree to work for no salary for a specific number of years because their employer has paid for their travel to a new country.

ore: naturally occurring mineral from which metals can by extracted.

smelt: the process of heating rock to remove the metal it contains.

Peter Cooper's train, *Tom Thumb.*

Until that moment, no one in America had seen a locomotive before. Although the invention had been around for some time in Europe, *Tom Thumb* was the first in the United States. It was built mostly out of iron, which inspired the nickname "iron horse."

At first, Lightning sprinted in front of the train. But as Cooper's locomotive built up a good head of steam, it began moving faster. Those who witnessed the race were amazed as *Tom Thumb* chugged down the tracks. As blue vapor spewed from *Tom Thumb's* smokestack, the locomotive's wheels spun wildly. The crowd shouted as Copper's iron horse slowly and steadily gained on the mare. Finally, the two were neck-and-neck, and then *Tom* passed the horse.

But suddenly, the locomotive's engine malfunctioned. The train slowed and allowed Lightning to gallop to victory. Many laughed at what was described as

Copper's "teakettle on a track." Still, within five years, there were more than 1,000 miles of railroad track in the United States, with more being built all the time. The iron horse was here to stay.

Old Metal

Iron is one of the oldest metals on the planet. Prehistoric people found they could use it for a variety of things, such as tools, weapons, and other objects. Pure iron, however, had limited uses. It was hard but brittle. To work iron into something more sturdy and useful, humans began to heat it at high temperatures.

We don't know when humans first learned how to **smelt** iron from **ore**, but most historians suspect it happened accidentally. Smelted ore could be shaped and hammered into spear points, axes, plows, and shovels. Before that period, humans

> ## Iron by the Numbers
>
> Atomic number: 26
> Atomic symbol: Fe
> Atomic weight: 55.845
> Phase at room temperature: solid
> Melting point: 2,800°F (1,538°C)
> Boiling point: 5,182°F (2,861°C)

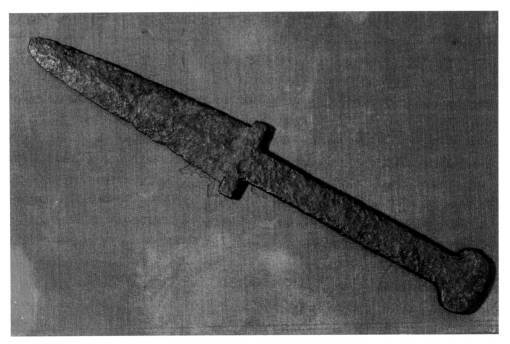

A knife from the Iron Age, discovered in Siberia, Russia.

Iron Age Timeline

1380 BCE: Hittite Empire begins working with iron.
1000 BCE: Iron working begins in Southern Europe.
750 BCE: Egypt begins using iron.
700 BCE: Iron is used throughout Europe.
650 BCE: Ironworking spreads to North Africa.

had used bones, rocks, and then bronze to make tools and weapons. Bronze, an **alloy** of copper, was very useful, but iron was better. It was strong and durable. Iron became so significant to human culture that historians now call this period the Iron Age.

Historians date the Iron Age to approximately 3,000 years ago, when the ancient Hittites, who lived in what is today Turkey and Syria, learned to make iron tools and weapons. Small amounts of steel were also used during the early part of the Iron Age. Steel is an alloy of iron. In fact, when Alexander the Great marched into India in 327 BC, he faced soldiers with steel weapons.

New World Iron

When European settlers came to the New World in the 1500s and 1600s, one of the first things they wanted to do was to find, mine, and refine iron ore. One of the earliest deposits the colonists found was in 1585 on an island off the North Carolina coast. The settlers of Jamestown found a deposit further inland and shipped several barrels of ore back to England in 1608.

In 1646, colonists built the first successful ironworks in North America on the banks of the Saugus River in Massachusetts. At the time, the colonists needed iron to build a variety of things, especially farm tools. By the mid-1640s, the Saugus Iron Works was pouring pig iron and forging wrought iron (see sidebar). At its peak in 1648, the ironworks employed 185 miners, ironworkers, woodcutters, and others.

By the end of the 1600s, a dozen ironworks existed in colonial New England. By the 1700s, the iron industry began to thrive, especially in Pennsylvania. When the American Revolution began in 1775, more than 70 furnaces and **forges** were in operation in Pennsylvania alone. It wasn't long before "Iron Plantations" began to pop up in the interior of America near waterways. The flowing water provided power for the sawmills, while the forests provided the fuel for the smelting furnaces.

Reconstruction of the water-powered forge at Saugus Iron Works, in Massachusetts.

Each plantation was self-sufficient. A typical iron plantation included general stores, blacksmith shops, gristmills, barns, orchards, smelters, and ovens. Skilled and unskilled workers, including **indentured servants** and slaves, worked the plantations. By the beginning of the American Revolution, the colonies had more iron furnaces in operation than in all of Britain, producing nearly 30,000 tons each year. The colonies exported much of that iron to Britain, and the English used it for shipbuilding and other things.

What's in a Name?

Iron goes by different names depending on how it is made:

- **cast iron**: iron with a high carbon content, often used in making cooking utensils such as pots and pans.
- **pig iron**: iron produced in a blast furnace and chiefly used in making steel.
- **wrought iron**: iron that is almost pure and contains less than 0.15 percent carbon, which makes it perfect for fences and stair cases.

Detail on a wrought iron fence.

Industrial Revolution

The widespread use of iron and steel really began during the early days of the Industrial Revolution, around the time *Tom Thumb* was trying to best Lightning. The Industrial Revolution was a period in history when many nations began to make the transition from farming societies to societies dominated by manufacturing and industry. The Industrial Revolution upended life as people knew it, resulting in fundamental changes in how they lived and worked. Increasingly, people could purchase the things they wanted, rather than making them at home. Instead, factories mass-produced many goods.

The Industrial Revolution could not have occurred without two key natural resources: iron and coal. Factories needed coal to fuel the iron steam engines that made machines run. By the mid-1800s, people were using steel more and more. Steel is iron that has been refined so it contains less than 1.7 percent carbon. Steel can be around 1,000 times stronger than pure iron. Steelmaking became a major industry in

The Boulton and Watt steam engine, from 1786. Businessman Matthew Boulton and inventor James Watt were central figures in the early years of the Industrial Revolution.

the United States during the late 1800s and early 1900s. Between 1880 and 1910, the production of steel skyrocketed from 1.4 million tons (1.27 million metric tons) to more than 28 million tons (25.4 million metric tons).

During and after World War II (1939–1945), the United Stated dominated the world's steel market. After the war, Germany and Japan were left in ruins. But in time, they began to rebuild their steel industries, using techniques and equipment that were more efficient than what US companies were using. In the 1970s, the production of US steel dropped, but production in other nations increased. People also began using less-expensive imported steel, as well as other alternatives, including plastic, to build things, such as cars and buildings. Today, US steel companies are not the industrial behemoths they once were. Most American steel companies have retooled and reorganized themselves to churn out specialized metal to make components for electronic equipment, such as computers, and other goods for industry.

TEXT-DEPENDENT QUESTIONS

1. How many years ago did the Iron Age begin?
2. Where was one of the first ironworks in Massachusetts located?
3. What is the different between cast iron and wrought iron?

RESEARCH PROJECTS

1. Create an inventory of the products made from iron or steel in your home or school.
2. Find a map of North America that you can copy or print out on a computer. Then research where the largest iron ore deposits are located. Plot the locations on the map. What can you conclude?

Chapter Two

EXTRACTION

Words to Understand

convection: circular motion of a liquid or gas resulting from temperature differences.

crust: the solid outer layer of Earth.

meteorite: a rock that has fallen to Earth from space.

Iron is the second most abundant metal on the planet (aluminum is the most abundant). However, pure iron is hard to find. That's because iron rapidly reacts with oxygen to form iron oxide, better known as rust. Moreover, most of the iron ore mined today is rust that has accumulated in ore. Extracting iron from ore is a time-consuming process, and most of it is done through mining. Processing iron ore into usable material also takes time.

Metal of Heaven

Our ancestors called iron "metal of heaven," and they weren't wrong. Most pure iron arrived on Earth inside rocky interstellar travelers called meteors. In fact, roughly 90 percent of a **meteorite** is pure iron. People in early civilizations who wanted to find the silver-gray metal, knew to look for craters on Earth's surface caused by falling meteorites. This is where our ancestors found the pure iron they needed to make tools and weapons.

Iron came to Earth when one or more massive stars exploded somewhere in the vast reaches of space. These stars were huge, more than eight times the size of our Sun. When a star uses up all its hydrogen and helium fuel, gravity begins to compress the core of the star. This compression creates a tremendous amount of heat, which forces different elements to change. For example, carbon turns into neon at 1,080 million degrees Fahrenheit (582 million degrees Celsius), while at 2,700 million degrees (1482

Close-up of a rock where the bands of iron are visible.

The Color of Rocks

The next time you go outside, peek at the color of the rocks and soil around you. Iron compounds are responsible for much of the color in the world's rocks. Deep red soil means that the iron was oxidized in hot conditions. Orange and yellow rocks were iron oxides that formed in cooler climates, while grays, blues, and greens were produced because iron compounds lacked oxygen (under the sea, for example. It's iron oxide that gives a reddish hue to the landscapes of Earth, such as in Australia, as well as other planets, like Mars.

The Red Rocks Canyon in Colorado takes its name from the color of the sandstone, which is caused by iron oxide.

million degrees Celsius), oxygen turns into silicon, and at 7,200 million degrees (3982 million degrees Celsius), silicon changes into iron.

Eventually, the star erupts in a blast , shining 100 million times more brightly than the Sun. The exploding star sends out trillions upon trillions of atoms of various elements into space, including iron, gold, and silver. All these elements showered down on Earth as it was forming.

Core Metal

Earth is made of three layers: the **crust**, the mantel, and the core. Over billions of years, iron atoms sank from the mantel to Earth's core, the planet's deepest layer. The outer core is composed of mostly liquefied iron and nickel. On Earth's surface, these metals are solid, but they form an alloy in the inner core. Earth's outer core is approximately 1,430 miles (2,300 kilometers) thick, and between 7,200 and 9,000°F (4,000 and 5,000°C).

Earth's 750-mile-thick (1,270 kilometer) inner core is made up mostly of solid iron. The pressure applied on the core by gravity is so great that iron cannot melt. Not all iron, however, is found in the center of the planet. When Earth was mostly covered by oceans, the iron compounds in the water settled to the ocean floors, mixing with sand and silt. Volcanic eruptions brought other iron ores violently to the surface, creating vast reservoirs of the metal.

Iron ore deposits are found around the world. In North America, the areas around the Great Lakes, including Minnesota, Michigan, and parts of Canada near Lake

Ferriferous sandstone, also known as iron ore.

Superior, are rich with iron ore. California, Missouri, and Wyoming also have large deposits, as does Labrador, Canada, and many parts of Mexico, especially in Sonora, Minatitlán, and Lázaro Cárdenas. Iron is usually found in combination with other elements, notably oxygen, carbon, sulfur, and silicon.

Iron ore comes in several main types: hematite, magnetite, limonite, siderite, and taconite. Hematite and magnetite contain 70 percent iron. Both are iron oxides, in which iron is bound with oxygen. Hematite is the most common ore and can be found in rocks that were once part of ancient rivers and oceans. Hematite is colored deep

Limonite in Arequipa, Peru.

Magnetic Personality

Iron is magnetic, as are iron alloys, such as steel. Iron has a magnetic quality because its tiny crystals organize themselves in the same direction. Iron is also the reason why Earth has a magnetic field. Scientists believe Earth's magnetic field is generated in its iron core. Remember, Earth's center is made up of a mostly solid inner core and a mostly liquid outer core. Heat radiated by the inner core causes the fluid in the outer core to expand and churn. As the liquid heats, its starts to rise. It then cools, and sinks down again. It's a process called **convection**. Convection generates an electrical current, which gives Earth its magnetic field.

red and found in warm climates. Limonite is also an iron oxide, but it forms in cooler regions. It is usually yellow, orange, or brown. It also contains water molecules, which can change the color of the rock.

Mining Iron

While some minerals are extracted from the Earth using underground mining techniques, iron is mined almost exclusively on the surface, although there is one underground iron mine in Missouri. Iron makes up about 5 percent of Earth's crust. The decision of whether to mine above or below ground depends on where iron deposits are located and on how close to the surface they are.

When miners find a surface deposit of iron ore, they remove layers of rock using power shovels, explosives and massive drilling machines. They then scoop out the ore and load it into trucks or railway cars so it can be carried away to be

World's Largest Open-Pit Iron Mine

The Hull Rust Mahoning Mine in Minnesota is the world's largest open-pit iron ore mine in the world. The mine is currently more than 3 miles (4.8 kilometers) long, more than 2 miles (3.2 kilometers) wide, and nearly 540 feet (165 meters) deep. The mine produces taconite, a low-grade iron. Since it started operation in 1895, miners have pulled more than 2 billion tons (1.8 billion metric tons) of ore from the pit.

Iron ore is loaded into trucks and hauled away for processing.

processed. Most open-pit mines yield high-grade ore, which usually contains about 52 percent iron.

Miners will also dig underground shafts and tunnels to reach the ore buried deep in the ground. Once the ore is brought to the surface, workers have to decide how pure it is. Miners can send high-grade ore directly to furnaces to be melted into crude iron. However, workers have to remove the impurities in low-grade ore before it can be made into useful products.

TEXT-DEPENDENT QUESTIONS

1. What is the difference between high-grade and low-grade iron ore?
2. What iron oxide forms in cooler regions?
3. Why does iron not melt in the Earth's core?

RESEARCH PROJECT

Research each layer of Earth's core. Keep in mind what each layer is made of and how deep it is. Once you are done with your research, write a short story about traveling to the center of the Earth. Your story should have a beginning, middle, and conclusion. You can create as many characters as you wish. Begin the journey at the crust and work your way down. What do you see? What is going on the deeper you go? Although this is a fictional story, be as factual as you can.

Chapter Three

SCIENCE AND USES

Words to Understand

chromium: a metallic element used in an alloy to increase hardness and corrosion resistance.

coke: carbon made by heating soft coal; also known as bituminous coal.

corrosion: the destruction of metal by various chemical processes.

electrodes: metal conductors through which electricity flows.

reducing agent: a substance that decreases another substance in a chemical reaction.

slag: waste material of smelting ore.

Thousands of years from now, if future archaeologists study our cities and towns, they'll find the crumpled remains of rusted-out bridges and buildings, cars and trucks, tools and airplanes, and ocean liners and tunnels. They will learn that our civilization depended on steel. Workers can forge steel, hammer it, bend it, and twist it into massive girders that weigh thousands of pounds or into wire so thin that it weighs next to nothing.

Steel is an alloy of iron and carbon that contains 50 percent or more iron and varying amounts of carbon (between 0.03 percent to about 2.25 percent). The amount of carbon determines the strength of the metal. More carbon increases steel's toughness, less carbon makes it weaker.

There are many kinds of steel. Workers can change the metal's structure by adding different elements to the alloy, such as **chromium**. Most types of steel fall into three categories: carbon, low alloy, and high alloy (stainless steel).

Once workers extract iron ore from the ground, it has to be processed before mills can turn the element into steel and other iron products. All of the impurities, such as phosphorus and sulfur, have to be eliminated from iron ore, or else the steel will be weak. To do that, the ore is smelted in a blast furnace that generates great heat.

The Gateway Arch in St. Louis, Missouri, is the largest stainless steel monument in the United States.

The Blast Furnace

When workers place iron ore in a furnace, they add a **reducing agent**, such as **coke**, to draw impurities, such oxygen, out of the ore. Coke is mostly carbon. Limestone is another element that helps remove impurities from iron ore. Limestone, one of the most common rocks on the planet, acts as a sponge, soaking up unwanted sulfur and phosphorus,

Smelting iron ore is a lot like baking a cake. Steel workers feed the ore, the coke, and the limestone into a furnace in carefully measured amounts. For each ton of iron, workers add about three-quarters of a ton of coke, and a quarter of a ton of limestone at specially timed intervals.

Many types of chemical reactions take place inside a blast furnace. Some reactions happen at the top, while others occur at the bottom. At the bottom of the furnace, workers feed oxygen through a ring of nozzles. When the oxygen and coke combine, they create carbon monoxide, a deadly gas. Carbon monoxide combines with iron

Iron in Your Body

Iron is very important to a person's health. It helps carry oxygen to your body's organs. Without enough iron, human organs can't function correctly. Lack of iron can cause a condition called iron-deficiency anemia, which can make a person very tired and weak. Foods such as red meat, fish, and beans are good sources of iron. Those who suffer from a lack of iron might have to take iron supplements to get the amount of iron they need.

Clams, oysters, and mussels are good sources of dietary iron—as are beef, veal, chicken, and other meats. Vegetarians can get their iron from beans, brussels sprouts, and raisins, among other sources.

Casting molten steel at a foundry.

On the Road

Steel slag is produced when impurities are removed during the steelmaking process. Steel slag can be recycled and used as an ingredient in road construction projects. About 8 million tons (7.5 million metric tons) of steel slag are recycled each year in the United States.

oxide, creating carbon dioxide gas. The carbon dioxide bubbles up through the furnace, reacting with more of the coke in the mixture, and creating more carbon monoxide. The gas then reacts with the iron oxide, which helps to produce liquefied iron. The molten iron, which is dense, moves toward the bottom of the furnace.

Every four or five hours, workers "tap" the molten iron and remove it from the furnace through an outlet on the side. The majority of the molten iron is transported in railway tanker cars and taken away so it can be turned into steel. Some of the iron, however, is poured into bars that can be used for other products. As workers drain the melted iron, known as pig iron, from the furnace, they also remove the less dense **slag**, the waste material produced when iron is separated from its ore, from another outlet.

Making Steel

Workers make steel in a few different ways: the Bessemer process, the basic oxygen process, the electric furnace process, and the open-hearth process. Regardless of the method, a batch of refined steel is called a *heat*.

The Bessemer process is the oldest steel-making method. Henry Bessemer invented the first steel furnace in the 1850s. Over the years, the Bessemer furnace, or converter, was modified and made more efficient.

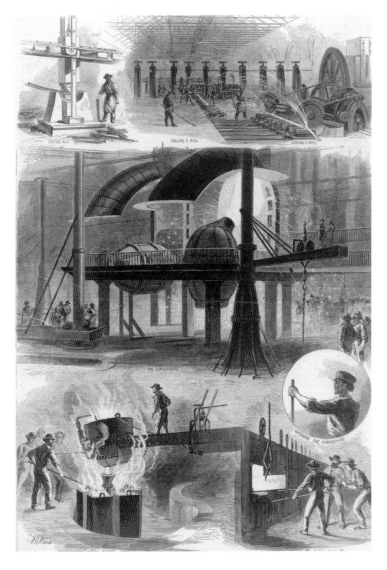

Illustrations from a magazine in 1876 depict the Bessemer steel-making process.

Most modern steel plants use basic oxygen technology, which allows workers to blow high-pressurized pure oxygen through the molten iron. The blown air causes the iron to oxidize, which creates a huge amount of heat. As the iron melts, the oxygen combines with impurities, creating waste gas that has to be vented and cleaned before being released into the environment. It also creates slag. When the process is complete, about 45 minutes later, workers tilt the furnace and pour molten steel into ladles.

Some steel mills use electric furnaces. Workers load the furnace with scrap iron and then lower large carbon **electrodes** to just above the surface of the metal. The electrodes never touch the iron. When a worker flips a switch that turns on the electricity, the gap between the electrodes and the iron creates a tremendously hot electrical arc. The arc is so hot and powerful that it melts the metal. This is how stainless steel and other high-quality metals are produced.

In the open-hearth process, workers put pig iron, limestone, and iron ore into an open hearth furnace. The furnace melts all the ingredients, allowing the slag that contains impurities to migrate out of the iron and float to the top of the melting iron broth.

Types of Steel

Some steel mills make low-carbon, or mild, steel. Low-carbon steel is one of the most widely used steels. It contains about 0.25 percent carbon. It can be easily twisted and bent, which makes it great for use in automobiles and household appliances. Mild steel can also be shaped when it is cooled.

Remember, workers can change steel's strength by altering the amount of carbon. The higher the carbon content, the stronger the steel. The strongest steel contains 0.6 to 2 percent carbon. Adding other materials, such as manganese and silicon, can also harden steel. Workers will often add chromium and nickel to improve steel's resistance to corrosion. Chromium steels are strong and hard. Factories use chromium steel to make tools, and cutlery. Common stainless steels are made with 18 percent chromium, 8 percent nickel, and 0.15 percent carbon.

Rust Never Sleeps

When you see something rusted, you're watching a chemical reaction take place. Rust, known as iron oxide, is a form of **corrosion**. When iron and oxygen meet, iron begins to corrode very slowly. However, if water is added, the process substantially quickens. When water hits a piece of iron, it combines with carbon dioxide in the air to form carbonic acid. The acid dissolves the iron. As that happens, some of the water breaks down into its constituent parts— oxygen and hydrogen. The oxygen and the dissolved iron bond, creating rust.

Some Uses of Iron and Steel

Iron and steel in all their forms are extremely useful. Iron chloride, a compound of iron and chlorine, is used in sewage treatment plants to treat polluted water. Iron hydroxide, a combination of iron, hydrogen, and oxygen, can help purify water, while iron arsenate is an ingredient in insecticides.

Wrought iron is nearly pure iron, which is soft. It can be worked by hand and made into rail fences, stairs, and garden gates. Wrought iron was once used to make railway tracks, until it was replaced by steel. The Eiffel Tower in Paris was fashioned out of wrought iron. Cast iron is iron that has been melted down and cooled, which makes it hard. Pots, pans, skillets, ovens, and other cooking utensils are forged from cast iron.

Still, no metal compares to steel in its toughness and in its variety of uses. It is used in making automobiles, trains, skyscrapers, bridges, guns, ships, and more. The Brooklyn Bridge, completed in 1883, was the first suspension bridge to use steel for its cable wire. The structure was the brainchild of the inventor and engineer John Roebling. Roebling wanted to construct two massive stone towers, over which workers would string four heavy steel cables. The Gateway Arch in St. Louis, Missouri, is also made from stainless steel siding. The arch, designed by Eero Saarinen, is 630 feet (192 meters) high and took nearly two years to build. It was completed in 1965.

The Empire State Building

The Empire State Building in New York City is one of the most iconic steel structures in the world. Workers needed 730 tons (662 metric tons) of aluminum and stainless steel to build the massive skyscraper. Each material added to the building's stability. Steel was used because it could withstand the push and pull a building so tall goes through. Workers put steel columns and beams inside the structure to create a stable grid.

The Empire State Building.

Many cooks like cast-iron pans because they are sturdy, versatile, and heat well.

No one wants to cut a piece of wood, a tomato, or a beard with a dull blade. That's why saw blades, knives, and razors are often made from an alloy called tungsten steel, which stays sharp for a long time. Another type of steel mentioned above, stainless steel, is also used in many household appliances. Stainless steel can also be made into sinks, faucet fixtures, and wire.

TEXT-DEPENDENT QUESTIONS

1. What are some of the uses of cast iron?
2. What is coke, and why do workers add the substance to a blast furnace?
3. How does rust form?

RESEARCH PROJECTS

1. Different environmental conditions can corrode metals at varying rates. Conduct these two simple experiments to test how fast metals corrode. Record your results.
2. Place several small nails in three cups of water. Put one teaspoon of salt in the first cup, two teaspoons of salt in second cup, and three teaspoons in the final cup. Leave the nails soaking over time. What happens? How does varying amounts of salinity cause metal to rust?
3. Look around and find strands of wire of different materials and thicknesses. Place each of the wires in two cups of vinegar or water. Place one cup in a cool, dry spot. Place the other cup in a warm spot. What happens to each of the wires? How does temperature affect corrosion? What can you conclude?

Chapter Four

COMMERCE AND ECONOMICS

F ew commodities influence a country's economic health more than iron and steel. The people of Youngstown, Ohio, know this from experience. From 1803, when James and Daniel Heaton found iron ore in Yellow Creek, up until the late 20th century, Youngstown was an important part of steelmaking in the United States. Thousands worked in the gigantic steel mills that called the iron-rich Mahoning River Valley home.

Words to Understand

burgeoning: growing.

profitable: yielding a financial profit.

recession: an economic downturn that is not as long as a depression.

As the United States prospered, so did Youngstown. For decades the blast furnaces burned day and night. The huge steel mills that towered over the city did everything in one place, from processing ore to making finished products. By the 1920s, the Mahoning River Valley and Youngstown were second only to Pittsburgh, Pennsylvania, in steelmaking. Youngstown boomed during World War II (1939–1945) when the military needed steel to build airplanes, tanks, aircraft carriers, and other tools of war.

By the early 1970s, however, the American steel market had collapsed. Extracting and processing high-grade ores became too expensive. Moreover, plastics

Part of the Republic Iron & Steel Company, in Youngstown, Ohio.

and other steel substitutes, along with less costly imported steel from Japan and other nations, decreased the demand for American steel. Youngstown and other steel cities became ghosts of their former selves.

The decline forced the steel industry to undergo an extreme makeover. Companies cut jobs, slimmed down, and retooled themselves to become more **profitable**. Labor contracts with union workers were renegotiated. The industry also began to make steels that are more specialized. New high-tech equipment and computers were used to forge the steel. It took years, but the American steel industry slowly dug itself out of its economic pit. After years of losing money, the 17 top steel companies had a combined profit of $6.6 billion in 2004.

Jobs Lost

On September 19, 1977, one of the largest steel mills in Youngstown closed, setting off a chain reaction that ultimately ended only after 10,000 jobs were eliminated between 1979 and 1981. Housing prices dropped. Tax dollars dried up. The city fell into economic oblivion. In the 1980s, Youngstown became synonymous with the decline of American industry, although it has slowly clawed its way back.

Economic Backbone

Steel and iron ore production is central to the economies of many nations, and is often considered an indicator of a country's financial health. The industry directly employs about 2 million workers worldwide, in addition to providing work for 2 million contractors and 4 million people in surrounding industries, including transportation and construction.

Like any other commodity, the price of iron ore and steel goes up and down with demand. As countries prosper, the demand for steel increases because consumers are buying more appliances and cars, while contractors are building new buildings. As countries deal with economic problems, the demand goes down. In the mid-2000s, the demand for steel increased as the economies of many countries, especially China, the world's largest producer and user of steel, did well. In countries such as China, India, and Brazil, workers built new bridges, roads, subways, and

Skyline of the Pudong district of Shanghai, China.

other projects that required a great amount of steel. By 2007, however, an economic slowdown (mainly in China), coupled with a worldwide steel glut, forced the cost of steel down. In 2014, the global demand for steel grew only 2 percent from the previous year.

Canadian Ore

Most of Canada's iron ore production is centered northeast Quebec and western Labrador, within a geological formation known as the Labrador Trough. Canada produces more than 33 million tons (30 million metric tons) of iron ore each year, most of which is exported to other countries.

Top 10 Steel-Producing Countries, 2012

1. China: 790 tons (716.5 metric tons)
2. Japan: 118.2 tons (107.2 metric tons)
3. United States: 97.7 tons (88.7 metric tons)
4. India: 85.5 tons (77.6 metric tons)
5. Russia: 77.6 tons (70.4 metric tons)
6. South Korea: 76.2 tons (69.1 metric tons)
7. Germany: 47 tons (42.7 metric tons)
8. Turkey: 39.5 tons (35.9 metric tons)
9. Brazil: 38 tons (34.5 metric tons)
10. Ukraine: 36.4 tons (33 metric tons)

For the most part, the steel industry in North America, especially in the United States, has done better since 2009. In the United States, steel production increased a whopping 6.7 percent increase in 2014 over the previous year, mainly because the country's automakers were building more cars and trucks.

Canton, Ohio, was one of the communities that reaped the benefits of the **burgeoning** American car industry. In 2009, at the height of a drawn-out **recession**, the town's steel mill was struggling. Orders dropped. The plant only operated four days a week. Then, in 2012, things changed dramatically. Demand for steel skyrocketed, and the mill began operating around the clock. Not only were American carmakers clamoring for more steel, but oil and natural gas companies needed specialized steel for drills, rigs, pipes, and other equipment. In fact, business was so good that the owners of the mill built a $200,000 million, 26-story addition to keep up with production. In Lorain, Ohio, the United States Steel Corporation opened a $100 million mill to make steel pipe, while in Youngstown, the poster child for a once battered and wrecked steel industry, a French company built a massive new pipe mill. Those and other projects were expected to add nearly 700 new manufacturing jobs to Ohio's economy in 2014. Moreover, the steel mills in Ohio were expected to produce 15 million tons (13.5 million metric tons) of steel in 2014, up from the 4.8 million tons (4.35 million metric tons) produced in 2009.

Important Commodity

Iron ore is the second most important commodity, next to crude oil, which is why iron is important to many state and local communities. This is especially true in Minnesota, which in 2012 produced 77 percent of the iron ore used in US steel mills.

Minnesota's iron ore industry is a $3-billion-a-year business, accounting for 5 percent of the state's economy. The industry provides work for 11,500 people. Almost all of Minnesota's production comes from open-pit mines on the Mesabi Iron Range.

The Largest Iron Ore Mines

Brazil has five of the world's largest iron ore mines, while Australia has six. The largest mine is the Carajás Mine, located in northern Brazil. The mine holds 8 billion tons (7.2 billion metric tons) of iron ore. The mine was discovered accidentally when a helicopter owned by US Steel had to make an emergency landing on a hill overlooking the area. The mine is a source of high-grade iron ore, with an iron content of nearly 66 percent.

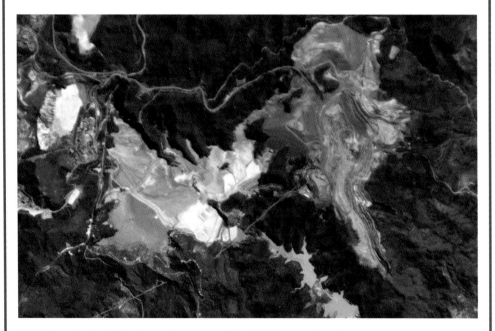

Satellite photo of the iron mine near Belo Horizonte, Brazil.

The Hull Rust Mahoning Mine, in Minnesota.

In 2013, mines in Michigan and Minnesota shipped 99 percent of the usable ore produced in the United States. The ore was valued at $5 billion.

But although iron ore remains central to Minnesota's economy, the area has not boomed as it did during the mid 20th century. During World War II, the mines of Minnesota's Mesabi Iron Range shipped more than 338 million tons (307 million metric tons) of ore. Although production remained high in the postwar period, it began to slack off in the 1960s and 1970s. Hoping to breathe new economic life into the mining industry, scientists at the University of Minnesota invented a process to mine low-grade taconite and concentrate the ore in pellets.

TEXT-DEPENDENT QUESTIONS

1. Which country is the top consumer of steel?
2. How do the laws of supply and demand affect the price of iron ore and steel?
3. Which state produces the most iron ore?

RESEARCH PROJECTS

1. Use the Internet or the library to research the global demand for iron ore and steel over the past decade. Create a line chart for each, and then compare the two. What can you conclude?
2. Research and create a chart of the top steelmaking countries in the world. Your chart should include the amount of steel each produces, how much steel each nation exports, and the amount of money the industry contributes to the national economy of each country.

Chapter Five

IRON AND THE ENVIRONMENT

Hamilton, Ontario, was once the hub of the Canadian steel industry. The town's economic life was centered on two giant mills that provided jobs for thousands of workers. Steelmaking began in Hamilton in 1892, and it ended in 2013, when the last mill locked its doors. Yet the legacy of steelmaking in this blue-collar city on the shore of Lake Ontario is still felt every time someone walks past the conglomeration of buildings and furnaces.

Words to Understand

biodegradable: the process by which bacteria and organisms naturally break down a substance.

heavy metals: metals such as mercury and copper that are often toxic to organisms.

hydrology: the study of the movement and distribution of water.

particulate: microscopic solids suspended in the air.

PCBs: acronym for polychlorinated biphenyls, dangerous industrial chemicals that are extremely toxic and an environmental hazard.

silica: a hard, white substance that is found in sand and other materials.

Industrial pollution is a big problem, but it is possible to trap the toxic chemicals before they are released into the air.

Over the past decade, the Canadian government has recorded 170 chemical, oil, and sewage spills, half of which occurred on land and half on water. The most recent mishap came in 2014, when 36 gallons (136 liters) of ammonia was spilled. Experts say the site is a toxic time bomb of **heavy metals**, oils, and cancer-causing **PCBs** (polychlorinated biphenyls). These and other materials are not **biodegradable** and can build up in the environment.

A Dirty Industry

Iron and steel production are both messy businesses. All of the steps in the process impact the environment. No one knows this better than the residents of the Monongahela River Valley, located about 10 miles (16 kilometers) from downtown

Pollution in Steeltown

Not long ago, Pittsburgh dominated the worldwide steel trade. But there was a price to pay. The city's steel factories and coke ovens, along with the burning of coal, made the city one of the most polluted places on the planet. The air in the 1950s and 1960s was so filthy that the city often had to keep its street lights on in the afternoon so people could see where they were going.

For the most part, people tolerated the soot and the health problems caused by the polluted air. Most of their livelihoods depended on the steel mills. Over the years, the air became cleaner as the city passed and enforced laws that required the burning of clean fuel. The

Close-up view of a blast furnace at the Pittsburgh Steel Company.

steel industry resisted many of these changes. However, by the 1970s and 1980s, new federal regulations, along with the decline of the steel industry, which shuttered most of the city's mills and ovens, helped make Pittsburgh's air breathable again.

The Carrie Blast Furnace in Pittsburgh is no longer used, but has been turned into a tourist attraction.

Pittsburgh. For decades, those living in the area sat downwind of the coke ovens that fed the city's appetite for steel.

Coke is produced by heating coal in an oven for 12 to 36 hours. It is one of the dirtiest industrial processes. The ovens contain a variety of noxious gases and dust, including sulfur and naphthalene, a chemical found in cigarette smoke and car exhaust. Unless the pollution caused by the coke ovens is neutralized, captured, or burned off, it is released into the air as exhaust. This is why the air over the Monongahela River Valley was brimming with pollution in 1995. Scientists found **particulate** matter so small that it could only be detected using an electron microscope. Today, because of new air-quality rules, the air is much cleaner, although in one local school district, half of the students are dealing with asthma, well above the national average. While US steel factories have cleaned up their act, many people complain that China's steel mills are polluting the environment.

Carbon Dioxide

Carbon dioxide is a major pollution problem in all steel plants. Steelmaking uses a lot of energy provided by fossil fuels, including oil and coal. According to the International Energy Agency (IEA), the steelmaking industry is responsible for generating about 30 percent of the world's carbon dioxide emissions. Carbon dioxide (CO_2) is a greenhouse gas that traps the Sun's heat near the Earth's surface, which scientists say causes global warming.

Moreover, the blast furnaces generate large amounts of noxious sulfur and nitrogen compounds, which pollute air and water. If these toxins—including heavy metals, acids, and phosphates—are not adequately removed or cleansed, they can cause serious environmental issues, such as the destruction of animal and plant life.

Over the years, the steel industry has made great strides in developing new techniques to control air and water pollution. Mills use sophisticated machines to scrub and filter waste gases before they are released. The water that the mills use to cool steel is also filtered before it leaves the plant.

Mexico's Steel Boom

In Mexico, steel factories have spent $3 billion to improve production to meet the demand of its auto industry. Mexico is an attractive nation for automakers because of low labor costs, and because Mexico can sell its steel in both North and South America. The demand for steel has made Mexico world's 13th largest steel-producing country.

Problems with Mining

The mining of iron ore is also a major concern for many municipalities, because of the widespread damage it can cause. In 2011 in Wisconsin, a Florida-based company proposed to dig the world's largest open-pit iron mine. According to 2012 report, the mine would create a heap of waste rock 500 feet (152 meters) high and 1.5 miles (2.4 kilometers) long over the 35-year life span of the mine. Moreover, researchers found that the mine would produce about 2.5 billion pounds (1.1 billion kilograms) of sulfur, created by the iron sulfide in the waste rock. When iron sulfide is exposed to air and water, it creates sulfuric acid, which could drain into the environment. Other heavy metals, such as arsenic, zinc, and copper could also poison the region. As of autumn 2014, the mine was still being debated.

Mining for iron can also influence an area's **hydrology**—the patterns of how water moves. As water seeps through the mines, ore piles, waste rock, or tailings (mine waste), it picks up contaminates. In some instances, water is exposed to sulfides, which combine with oxygen and a certain acid-loving bacteria in the ground. When that happens, a type of pollution known as acid mine drainage (AMD) is created.

An extreme example of acid mine pollution in Romania.

As its name suggests, AMD is highly acidic. It can kill plants and animals and ruin ecosystems. Often, a stream or pond will turn red because of AMD. In addition, production of AMD can occur long after the mines have been abandoned.

Working with iron ore can also make people sick, whether they are mining, crushing, or smelting the rock. Iron ore is crammed with impurities that include quartz, lime, magnesium, sulfur, copper, arsenic, and other substances. When the ore is mined and processed, it creates tiny dust particles that a person can inhale. As a result, a person can suffer from a variety of lung diseases, including cancer, which is mainly caused by **silica** in the dust. Silica can cause silicosis, a chronic lung disease marked by a shortness of breath. Exposure to iron ore dust can also cause a flu-like illness, with fever, chills, chest tightness, and coughing.

Caverns and Earthquakes

Like any underground mine, an underground iron mine can reshape the geology and geography of the land even after the mine has closed. For example, the mineshafts underneath Moriah, New York, continued to impact the lives of people in the area years after mining ended.

From 1820 to 1971, the iron miming industry flourished in Moriah. High-grade iron ore was mined in deep tunnels near the tiny hamlets of Mineville and Witherbee, and transported south by train to the steel mills. Long after the mines closed, however, craters began to appear, some more than 100 feet (30 meters) deep. Several of the mineshafts had been capped after the last of the ore was extracted in the 1970s, but rainwater and time reopened many of the holes. In the 1980s, people grew concerned that their homes would be swallowed by sinkholes.

Moreover, earthquakes in Witherbee—strong enough to crack home foundations, toss dishes from the shelves, and force people out of their beds at night—rattled the region more than a decade after the mines closed. At the time, scientists said that the mineshafts underneath the village were filling up with water, causing the earth to shake. The flooding weakened not only the underlying rock, but also the naturally occurring fault lines.

The earthquakes have since stopped, but the people in Moriah still have fond memories of the iron ore days that put their community on the map. The slag piles were always looked upon as a badge of honor. As with other mining communities throughout North America, mining iron ore and steelmaking were sources of pride. In some towns, the remnants of old furnaces, such as those in Roxbury, Connecticut,

Boys as young as 12 or 13, working an iron mine in Tennessee. Photographed by Lewis Hine in 1910.

Close-up of a slag pile in Massachusetts.

are historical sites where tourists can learn how iron was processed and made into such things as cannon balls, cannons, hulls of ships, and pots and pans.

Although the mining and processing of iron is nowhere near what it has been in the past, especially in the United States, the world still craves iron. Many emerging economies, including China and India, thirst for the metal as they seek to improve life for their citizens by building new buildings, roads, bridges, and other structures. Iron still plays a vital role in society, as it long has and probably always will.

TEXT-DEPENDENT QUESTIONS

1. How does AMD form?
2. How can an area's hydrology affect an ecosystem?
3. How do coke ovens cause air pollution?

RESEARCH PROJECT

Air pollution is a very real problem in many communities. To see how big of a problem it is your town or neighborhood, find some duct tape, five index cards, and petroleum jelly. Smear the petroleum jelly on the cards, and tape the cards to various surfaces, such as the side of a building, the blackboard in your classroom, a tree trunk, your kitchen, or outside your front door. Label each of the cards with its location. After a day or two, retrieve the cards. What do you see? What can you conclude about air pollution in each of these locations? What generalizations can you make?

"To waste, to destroy, our natural resources, to skin and exhaust the land instead of using it so as to increase its usefulness, will result in undermining in the days of our children the very prosperity which we ought by right to hand down to them amplified and developed."

—Theodore Roosevelt
President of the United States (1901 to 1909)
Seventh Annual Message
December 3, 1907

Further Reading

BOOKS

Collis, John. *The European Iron Age.* Reprint. London: Routledge, 1997.

Gray, Theodore. *The Elements: A Visual Exploration of Every Known Atom in the Universe.* Reprint. New York: Black Dog & Leventhal, 2012.

Hason, Heather. *Iron.* Understanding the Elements of the Periodic Table. New York: Rosen, 2005.

Hoerr, John P. *And the Wolf Finally Came: The Decline and Fall of the American Steel Industry.* Pittsburgh Series in Social and Labor History. Pittsburgh, PA: University of Pittsburgh Press, 1988.

Misa, Thomas J. *A Nation of Steel: The Making of Modern America, 1865–1925.* Baltimore, MD: Johns Hopkins University Press, 1995.

Reutter, Mark. *Making Steel: Sparrows Point and the Rise and Ruin of American Industrial Might.* Urbana: University of Illinois Press, 2004.

ONLINE

British Broadcasting Corporation, "Iron Age Life." http://www.bbc.co.uk/history/ancient/british_prehistory/launch_gms_ironage_life.shtml.

Minnesota Department of Environmental Resources. "Minnesota Mining History." http://www.dnr.state.mn.us/education/geology/digging/history.html.

Minnesota Museum of Mining. http://www.ironrange.org/things-to-do/minnesota-museum-of-mining.

Natural Resources Canada. http://www.nrcan.gc.ca/home.

Series Glossary

alloy: mixture of two or more metals.

alluvial: relating to soil that is deposited by running water.

aquicludes: layers of rocks through which groundwater cannot flow

aquifer: an underground water source.

archeologists: scientists who study ancient cultures by examining their material remains, such as buildings, tools, and other artifacts.

biodegradable: the process by which bacteria and organisms naturally break down a substance.

biodiversity: the variety of life; all the living things in an area, or on Earth on the whole.

by-product: a substance or material that is not the main desired product of a process but happens to be made along the way.

carbon: a pure chemical substance or element, symbol C, found in great amounts in living and once-living things.

catalyst: a substance that speeds up a chemical change or reaction that would otherwise happen slowly, if at all.

commodity: an item that is bought and sold.

compound: two or more elements chemically bound together.

constituent: ingredient; one of the parts of a whole.

contaminated: polluted with harmful substances.

convection: circular motion of a liquid or gas resulting from temperature differences.

corrosion: the slow destruction of metal by various chemical processes.

dredge: a machine that can remove material from under water.

emissions: substances given off by burning or similar chemical changes.

excavator: a machine, usually with one or more toothed wheels or buckets that digs material out of the ground.

flue gases: gases produced by burning and other processes that come out of flues, stacks, chimneys, and similar outlets.

forges: makes or shapes metal by heating it in furnaces or beating or hammering it.

fossil fuels: sources of fuel, such as oil and coal, that contain carbon and come from the decomposed remains of prehistoric plants and animals.

fracking: shorthand for hydraulic fracturing, a method of extracting gas and oil from rocks.

fusion: energy generated by joining two or more atoms.

geologists: scientists who study Earth's structure or that of another planet.

greenhouse gas: a gas that helps to trap and hold heat—much like the panes of glass in a greenhouse.

hydrocarbon: a substance containing only the pure chemical substances, or elements, carbon and hydrogen.

hydrologic cycle: events in which water vapor condenses and falls to the surface as rain, snow, or sleet, and then evaporates and returns to the atmosphere.

indigenous: growing or living naturally in a particular region or environment.

inorganic: compound of minerals rather than living material.

kerogens: a variety of substances formed when once-living things decayed and broke down, on the way to becoming natural gas or oil.

leachate: liquid containing wastes.

mineralogists: scientists who study minerals and how to classify, locate, and distinguish them.

nonrenewable resources: natural resources that are not replenished over time; these exist in fixed, limited supplies.

ore: naturally occurring mineral from which metal can be extracted.

ozone: a form of oxygen containing three atoms of oxygen in a molecule.

porous: allowing a liquid to seep or soak through small holes and channels.

primordial: existing at the beginning of time.

producer gas: a gas created ("produced") by industrial rather than natural means.

reclamation: returning something to its former state.

reducing agent: a substance that decreases another substance in a chemical reaction.

refine: to make something purer, or separate it into its various parts.

remote sensing: detecting and gathering information from a distance, for example, when satellites in space measure air and ground temperature below.

renewable: a substance that can be made, or a process used, again and again.

reserves: amounts in store, which can be used in the future.

runoff: water not absorbed by the soil that flows into lakes, streams, rivers, and oceans.

seismology: the study of waves, as vibrations or "shaking," that pass through the Earth's rocks, soils, and other structures.

sequestration: storing or taking something to keep it for a time.

shaft: a vertical passage that gives miners access to mine.

sluice: artificial water channel that is controlled by a value or gate.

slurry: a mixture of water and a solid that can't be dissolved.

smelting: the act of separating metal from rock by melting it at high temperatures

subsidence: the sinking down of land resulting from natural shifts or human activities.

sustainable: able to carry on for a very long time, at least the foreseeable future.

synthesis: making or producing something by adding substances together.

tailing: the waste product left over after ore has been extracted from rock.

tectonic: relating to the structure and movement of the earth's crust.

watercourse: a channel along which water flows, such as a brook, creek, or river.

Index

(page numbers in *italics* refer to photographs and illustrations)

About the Author

John Perritano is an award-winning journalist, writer, and editor from Southbury, Connecticut. He has written numerous articles and books on history, culture, and science for publishers that include National Geographic's Reading Expedition Series and its Global Issues Series. He has also contributed to Discovery.com, *Popular Mechanics,* and other magazines and Web sites. He holds a master's degree in American history from Western Connecticut State University.

Photo Credits

Cover
Clockwise from left: Dollar Photo Club/simonlaprida; iStock.com/rja; iStock.com/mypokcik; Dollar Photo Club/Tomasz Bidermann; Dollar Photo Club/jovannig; Dollar Photo Club/sorapolujjin; Dollar Photo Club/waldemarus.

Interior
Dollar Photo Club: 14 drutska; 20 nstanev; 27 clearviewstock; 28 dulsita; 33 re_production; 34 MasterLu; 35 minadezhda.
iStock.com: 11 LuVo; 21 FokinOl; 24 SergeyZavalnyuk; 29 OlegFedorenko; 30 wabeno; 40 zoom-zoom; 46 ErikdeGraaf; 48 brandonhirtphoto; 50 -Oxford-; 51 alexandrumagurean.
Library of Congress: 10; 31 A.R. Waud; 38 Jay Williams; 47 Jet Lowe; 53 Lewis Wickes Hine.
Wikimedia Commons: 13 Daderot; 15 Tony Hisgett; 19 Wilson44691; 22 Rojinegro81; 42 Planet Labs Inc.; 43 Chipcity; 54 Marc N. Belanger.